Live Generously!

Responding to God's Call to Give to Him
As We Trust in His Provision for Us

Anthony Shannon

renownpublishing

Renown Publishing

Live Generously! / Anthony Shannon
ISBN-13: 978-1-945793-67-7
ISBN-10: 1-945793-67-8

I dedicate this project:

To the Shannon family—Glynis, AJ, Kendra, and Ba'lint. Your faith in my leadership of our family has taught me the greatest possible lessons of faith in my heavenly Father. Thank you for all your support of my ministry activities.

To my mother, Sharon Shannon, and my grandmother, Jennie Lowe, whose steadfast faith in God through the many trials and challenges of raising respectable and successful children and grandchildren has inspired me to believe that nothing is ever impossible.

To Bishop William H. Murphy Jr., whose commitment to God and demonstration of prayer and worship in exceptional faith, in the face of tremendous personal pain and loss, gives me the impetus to face my future with stainless confidence that I can do all things through Jesus Christ.

To Victory Church International and my brother, Arnold D. Shannon, for believing in the revelation of seedtime and harvest and getting results from God through giving. May this book become a source of encouragement and fuel your faith to believe in a better tomorrow by Living Generously.

To the author and finisher of my faith, Jesus Christ. Thank You for having enough faith in me to die to restore my faith in You— and for calling me to work in the Kingdom of God. You have made my life so enriched, and now You are drawing out the author in me. I give you all glory and honor for the things You have done in my life.

CONTENTS

Foreword by Dr. R. A. Vernon

There are tons of books about money. What differentiates *Live Generously!* from other finance books is that Pastor Shannon is more interested in reframing conceptions about money than telling readers exactly what to do with it. This is a decidedly more helpful approach since, as Pastor Shannon puts it, "We all bristle at the prospect of telling another person what to do with their money, the same way we would if someone else told us what to do with ours."

He addresses the primary reasons behind why people don't give, which—we learn upon closer examination—are rooted mainly in self-preservation. Then, he uses examples from Scripture and personal anecdotes to answer these concerns.

With theological mindfulness, he recasts commonly misconstrued terms such as tithing, favor,

4 · ANTHONY SHANNON

prosperity, and God's abundance with sharper focus, clearing up flawed definitions and replacing them with substantive explanations. Readers will find resonance in the reflection of their own misgivings about money—and solace in the solutions provided.

The questions at the end of every chapter help to extract even more meaning from the text. They are worded in ways that encourages deeper thought and intellectual interaction with what has been written.

If you want to experience financial peace and are willing to embrace a fresh mindset about money, then the book you hold in your hands is the passport to your destination.

R. A. Vernon, D.Min.
Founder and Senior Pastor, The Word Church
www.wordcity.org

Foreword by
Bishop William H. Murphy Jr.

Wow! is the word that comes out of my spirit after reading Prophet Anthony Shannon's revelation on money—*Living Generously!*

The words here represent the very essence of how the Father desires and wants us to operate and deal with the money that He places in our hands.

Biblical truth, as well as doctrinal new truth, is always important in the how we release our thoughts and revelations with which we minister to others. I believe that the word Prophet Shannon shares and releases to us is well on target with what the Spirit of the Lord would say to His people in this season. As soon as I started reading, many of the traditional, religious thoughts of my past were confronted.

This is because Prophet Shannon, with much tact, exposes many of the tricks and strategies that the enemy uses against believers to keep them broke, in lack, and in poverty. He also exposes many of the hidden spirits that the enemy has used, and is using, against believers in spiritual warfare over money.

My prayer for all who come across this book is that they would take the time to read its contents carefully because this is a teaching that the church of God needs in this season in order to prepare for the in-time harvest.

I believe personally that as we prepare for this harvest, God will raise up individuals that to uniquely finance its coming. This means that every believer, every church member, must be positioned in mind and in spirit to give to the best of his or her ability to make it happen. That's why the message of this book is a necessary teaching.

The money wisdom of sowing and reaping released to us here is of such powerful truth that those who read it will certainly be transformed into this new thing God is doing and releasing in this last day.

Interceding for you,

Bishop William H. Murphy Jr.
Senior Pastor of New Mount Moriah
Pontiac, Michigan

INTRODUCTION

A Great Taboo

Our churches are safe spaces—places where people can gather without fear and hear God's Word on all kinds of important issues. The Bible does not shy away from any topic; nothing is off-limits, because nothing can be hidden from God. This might make us nervous to think about, but it's a good thing: God knows us better than anyone, even the worst parts of us, and He loves us regardless. Why then should we feel ashamed to talk about anything and everything in His house?

But we often are ashamed when certain topics come up. Preachers address all sorts of difficult subjects: crises of faith, sin, and even sex, but they often stumble when the conversation comes around to money. There are many reasons for this, of course, and some of them are perfectly reasonable.

Most of us don't have as much money as we want; *many* of us don't even have as much money as we need. Setting these realities aside doesn't make the conversation any easier. We all bristle at the prospect of telling another person what to do with their money, the same way we would if someone else told us what to do with ours. In some ways, money has become our last great taboo.

Yet financial concerns remain an essential part of our everyday lives. No matter how much some of us love our jobs, there's no getting around the fact that we work so we can live. In today's world, money is as necessary for survival as the air we breathe. If you don't believe me, try getting by without either.

God understands the importance of money, which is why it's discussed, in one way or another, throughout the Bible. There are 500 verses on prayer, and fewer than 500 on faith, but more than 2,000 verses dealing with the subject of money. One out of every seven verses in the New Testament deals with money. It's the main subject of nearly half of the parables Jesus told.[1]

This means that we can look to God's Word for guidance, just as we would with any difficult subject. But doing so requires facing certain uncomfortable truths. When God asks us to get our houses in order, He sometimes means our *literal* homes (2 Kings 20:1). When we do, we may discover that, at times, we prioritize material things and comforts while neglecting charity and even our own church communities.

Imagine a parishioner from your local church, a woman named Lucy around the same age as yourself. Lucy receives $1,000 she didn't expect back from her taxes. She's thrilled as she considers what to do with this windfall. First, she decides to pay a bill or two. Then, because she's a sweet, family-oriented person, Lucy sends some money home to her parents. She's also smart about money, so she tucks some of the rest into her savings. So far, so good.

Lucy still has some cash left, so she decides to go shopping, first for some items she needs and then just for some stuff she likes. That pool of money is almost gone by the time Sunday rolls around, but she manages to drop the last dollar into the collection basket.

We aren't here to judge Lucy—or anyone else—because we haven't walked a mile holding her purse. We can still use this example to look at our own attitudes and behaviors. Money can be used or invested in any number of ways, but it is important to take a look at what the Bible says about the way we should handle ours.

In the following pages, we will examine what the Bible teaches us about giving and living generously for His kingdom and tithing regularly to the church. And at the end of each chapter, an application-focused workbook section will help you begin practicing these truths in your daily life—not just when the offering plate is passed around on Sunday.

Are you ready to take a leap of faith and express your trust in the God who provides? Read on and discover why giving is an essential part of the life of every Christian.

WORKBOOK

Introduction Questions

Question: Why do you think money is often a taboo subject in Christian churches?

_____

_____

_____

_____

_____

_____

_____

_____

_____

_____

Question: Where do you look for financial advice? Is the Bible on your list—and why or why not?

_____

_____

_____

_____

_____

_____

_____

_____

_____

_____

_____

Action: If you were to receive an unexpected $1,000, how would you spend it? Make a list and evaluate to what extent your expenditures would be based on God's priorities or your own.

_____

_____

_____

_____

_____

_____

Introduction Notes

_____

_____

_____

_____

_____

_____

_____

_____

_____

_____

_____

_____

_____

_____

_____

_____

_____

_____

_____

_____

CHAPTER ONE

Which God Do You Serve?

Early in the Gospel of Matthew, Jesus and His apostles climbed to the top of a mountain as a huge crowd of people gathered below to hear Him preach. He then delivered one of His most famous sermons, part of which many probably know by heart: "Blessed are the poor in spirit, for theirs is the kingdom of heaven. Blessed are those who mourn, for they will be comforted. Blessed are the meek, for they will inherit the earth" (Matthew 5: 3–5).

We tend to focus on the Beatitudes because they sound like poetry, but later in the Sermon on the Mount, Jesus said something just as important: "No one can serve two masters; for either he will hate the one and love the other, or else he will be loyal to the one and despise the other. You cannot serve God and mammon" (Matthew 6:24 NKJV).

Now, *mammon* is an old-fashioned word for greed. There are many words for greed, some of them very old, because that vice has been around as long as people have walked this earth. Greed means wanting to *take, take, take*, and after taking, to keep as much as you possibly can. It doesn't matter if the taking involves grain or livestock, as it did back in those times, or if it involves the paper money we use today. Since the beginning, human beings have always wanted *more,* or even *all* if they can arrange it. And whatever money or possessions they succeed in getting, they are very reluctant to part with.

That may be man's way, but it's certainly not God's. In fact, the Bible asks us to share what we have been blessed with. In 2 Corinthians 9:7, Paul writes, "Each of you should give what you have decided in your heart to give, not reluctantly or under compulsion, for God loves a cheerful giver."

"Cheerful giving" seems like a very strange idea, maybe even a crazy one. Why would we give away what we have worked so hard to gain for ourselves? And if we do give it away, why on earth should we be *happy* about it? Our difficulty in understanding this phrase comes from the way we look at money. Our lives are a series of calculations with money at the root: *How much do groceries cost? What would a new car cost? How much will buying this home cost?*

To give to our church or a charity doesn't have

the same cause-and-effect relationship that we typically replay in our minds: *I pay this to get that.* In fact, it can feel an awful like "throwing money away," because we don't see an immediate benefit. But that doesn't mean there isn't one. In Matthew's retelling of the Sermon on the Mount, Jesus wasn't simply warning against putting our pursuit of wealth over God in our lives; He was reminding His audience, including us, that there's a big difference between the material world of man and the Kingdom of God.

In our world, money means survival at the very least, or even comfort when spent well. But it can also lead to dissatisfaction, or worse, greed when we focus too much on the trivialities of the material world. In the same way that we may review our finances, from time to time we need to examine our other "portfolio" Are we neglecting charity and our church? Charitable giving is like a deposit in a spiritual retirement account—one with a much better return on our investment!

It is important to understand the types of giving. These include spontaneous, systematic, sacrificial, sovereign, and strategic giving.

Tithing: Recognizing What Is God's

"Bring the whole tithe into the storehouse, that there may be food in my house. Test me in this," says the LORD Almighty, "and see if I will not throw open the floodgates of heaven and pour

out so much blessing that there will not be room enough to store it."

—Malachi 3:10

People often think of a tithe as a "God tax" or an arrangement in which they are somehow paying Him rent. This way of thinking can lead to confusion. When we hear "A tithe is ten percent of what you earn" (see Deuteronomy 14:22–26), it's hard not to think of God as an IRS agent, requiring us to pay a portion of everything we own and punishing us if it isn't paid in a certain way and at a certain time. In truth, though, a tithe is just a sign of our appreciation for God's blessings in our lives. We offer a portion of what we have as a way of recognizing that *everything* we have flows from Him. By tithing, we are, in essence, thanking God for those blessings.

Where does the number, this ten percent, come from? That question reminds me of my time as a student at Eastern Kentucky University. God has granted me many gifts in life, but math skills are definitely not among them. I struggled with the subject as far back as high school, partly because I didn't try as hard as I should have. My wife told me when she needed to pass a statistics course in college, she took the class twice and always ran up against the same trouble: she needed to understand the why for every equation and formula. She couldn't move forward until I understood the why.

Luckily, God made up for not making her a math genius by putting the right person in her path. During her college years, she worked as an office assistant in one of the departments to pay her tuition. Her office partner was a former notorious drug dealer who had just been released from federal prison. When she met him, he still wore the tether around his ankle.

Yet, whatever bad decisions he had made in his life, he was no slouch when it came to math. Algebra, statistics, and equations all came very easily to him, and before long, he explained her problem to her. Willy said, "What you need to know about math is, it's just rules. You are trying to understand it when you really just need to accept it."

For some reason, that answer cleared the fog for her, and she ended up finally passing the class. His words are just as useful when it comes to understanding the principle of tithing. Giving doesn't always make sense; it especially doesn't make sense when we don't have much to begin with. But the Word of God isn't always supposed to make sense to us. Proverbs 3:5–6 says, "Trust in the LORD with all your heart; do not depend on your own understanding. Seek his will in all you do, and he will show you which path to take" (NLT).

Put even more simply, as the wise Willy Brown told me back in college, "Trust the rule (and trust

God)."

Why We Don't Give

Most people are not givers. Some might like to give, but they hold back out of fear of worsening their difficult circumstances: *I barely have enough to survive, so how can I give to anyone else?* It's easy to understand this dilemma, but the truth is, that situation doesn't apply to all of us.

We often maintain the very selfish mind-set of someone with a Scrooge mentality—we want to hoard everything we have for ourselves. We aren't born with this attitude, but we tend to learn it over time. Part of the reason for this is that we aren't taught properly about money. For all the time we spend in school as children, precious little of it is spent on the topic of finances. There are history and science and English classes, but few on budgeting or balancing a bank account or practical matters of that nature.

Students today would benefit if some consumer math topics such as budgeting, taxes, credit cards, understanding bank statements, and even grocery shopping were included in curriculums. Part of learning about money is learning to work with and be content with what we have—regardless of the amount of our salary. Some of us are lucky enough to get taught the basics by our parents or relatives, but the majority of people don't know anything about money.

Often, what we do learn comes from bad sources that influence our thinking in ways we might not even realize. There are countless news articles, shows, and radio and television commercials devoted to the success stories of those who supposedly found wealth by investing in this project or that technology. Sometimes it seems like everyone in the whole world is engaged in the exact same pursuit: getting as rich as possible, as quickly as possible.

All of this exposure fills in the gaps in our understanding. But all it really does is bring about discontent, not truly show us how to be good stewards of what God has provided to us. Greed settles in our brains like a virus and just grows bigger. Before we didn't know anything about money, but now our thinking goes something like this: *Give me what you've got and let me keep what I've got.* If we are focused on how much money we can gain for ourselves, then there's not a whole lot of room for giving, much less God, in that perspective. The greed virus continues to affect our actions.

Greed

The Bible tells of the dangers of such thinking in Acts 5:1–5. This passage tells the story of Ananias and Sapphira, a married couple who sold some property for a great deal of money. However, they allowed greed to slip in and cloud their thinking. Their greed led to lies.

When the church was growing in Acts, the believers were giving sacrificially, "All the believers were together and had everything in common. They sold property and possessions to give to anyone who had need" (Acts 2:44–45).

However, when Ananias and Sapphira sold their property—they wanted to have the appearance of being generous while secretly keeping a portion back for themselves (Acts 5:1–2). This greedy couple dropped their sacrifice at Peter's feet and claimed that was the entire portion. Peter sniffed out the scam almost instantly.

"Ananias," Peter said, "why have you let Satan fill your heart? You lied to the Holy Spirit, and you kept some of the money for yourself" (NLT). In other words, Peter asked, "Why did you violate your promise? Why is it so important that you keep some for yourself while pretending like you are giving everything? Why are you hesitant to live generously when all your blessings come straight from God?"

We all have our own reasons for withholding from God. We may not be as deceitful as Ananias and Sapphira, but it's also true that we aren't all afraid of being left destitute, either.

Fear

Some of us don't give because we fear persecution or ridicule from our friends and neighbors.

People who are caught up in the material world don't always look kindly on those who offer tribute to God's kingdom. As backward as it may sound, to spend money on the latest big-screen TV seems a lot more sensible to some than offering money to God.

Distrust

Others among us don't necessarily trust that their tithe will be put to good use. They've learned to distrust authority figures, and whether it's fair or not, that list has grown to include their church leaders. But we need to remember that God calls us to give to Him as a representation of our trust in *His provision for us.*

If we know for certain that church leaders are dishonest with the tithes and offerings, then we should still direct our tithes elsewhere until the situation is resolved. However, if we withhold our tithes altogether because of a general—perhaps even misplaced—distrust, then we are showing a lack of faith and are being disobedient.

None of these reasons should affect our faith in God, the trust in Him that a tithe represents. Nor should they be used as excuses to avoid offering back some of the harvest He has granted to us. We have no reason to doubt God. When we tithe, we are acknowledging that it all belongs to Him anyway, and that we are trusting that He will not punish us financially for our faith.

WORKBOOK

Chapter One Questions

Question: Why do people sometimes feel that giving to church or another ministry is throwing their money away? Which Scripture verses address this mindset?

_____

_____

_____

_____

_____

_____

_____

_____

_____

_____

Question: What attitudes should accompany tithing? What attitudes should not?

_____

_____

_____

_____

_____

_____

_____

_____

_____

_____

_____

Question: What are some reasons people don't give? Which rationale (or excuse) poses the greatest struggle for you? How does tithing demonstrate faith?

_____

_____

_____

_____

_____

_____

_____

_____

_____

_____

_____

_____

Action: For a week (or a pay period), keep track of where *all* of your money is spent. Then divide into major headings such as "Food," "Utilities," "House," "Entertainment," etc. Note beside each expenditure if it was a *need* or a *want*. Would you say that you are serving God or money?

Chapter One Notes

_____

_____

_____

_____

_____

_____

_____

_____

_____

_____

_____

_____

_____

_____

_____

_____

_____

_____

_____

_____

_____

CHAPTER TWO

God Can Be Trusted

In 1 Kings 17:7–24, God commanded Elijah to travel to Zarephath, a small village suffering through a crippling drought, where a widow would feed him. There, the hungry prophet met a widow and asked her for some water and bread. But the widow herself was starving because the drought had led to a terrible famine in the region. She explained to Elijah that she had neither water nor bread to offer, only a little olive oil and flour, which she had planned to use to make a last meal for her and her son. This is how Elijah responded:

> *Elijah said to her, "Don't be afraid. Go home and do as you have said. But first make a small loaf of bread for me from what you have and bring it to me, and then make something for yourself and your son. For this is what the LORD, the God of Israel, says: 'The jar of flour will not be used up and the jug of oil will not run dry until the day the*

LORD sends rain on the land.'"

—1 Kings 17:13–14

Even though the widowed mother was starving and facing death, she faithfully did as she was told, and just as Elijah promised, there was enough flour and olive oil for all three of them to eat: "For the jar of flour was not used up and the jug of oil did not run dry, in keeping with the word of the LORD spoken by Elijah" (1 Kings 17:16).

Sometime later, however, the widow's boy became ill and stopped breathing. In her grief, the widow lashed out at Elijah: "What do you have against me, man of God? Did you come to remind me of my sin and kill my son?" (1 Kings 17:18).

Elijah was just as distraught. He took the lifeless boy, placed him on his bed, and cried, "LORD my God, have you brought tragedy even on this widow I am staying with, by causing her son to die?" (1 Kings 17:20).

God heard Elijah's words and saved the boy. The widow was beside herself with relief. She told Elijah, "Now I know that you are a man of God and that the word of the LORD from your mouth is the truth" (1 Kings 17:24).

In a moment of grief, this heartbroken mom wavered in her faith. She had already seen God use Elijah to miraculously feed her and her son. Sometimes people waver in their faith, or when they see God come through, they feel their faith strengthened even more, just as the widow felt such relief. She gave God all the credit and glory and recognized that Elijah was His prophet because of what he had done.

The Bible is full of such tales, stories of people who see their faith in God rewarded. We can also look back on our own lives and find similar experiences, even though they may be less dramatic than God bringing back a loved one from the dead.

I have a married friend who lives in Atlanta. He's a good man, but for a long time he favored a certain type of lifestyle—clubbing and drinking. His wife had no interest in those things. It created a lot of problems in their relationship. They fought constantly, and when she accepted Christ, things got even worse. So, this woman turned to God. She said, "I'm going to entrust him to You, Lord, that You might change his behavior and change him into the kind of man I need."

One day a few months later, my friend came home from another late night to see his wife praying for him. He was blown away by the gesture, by her faith. That night, he got down on his knees when she went to sleep and asked God to deliver him. And God did. The couple is still married to this day, and they spend their time traveling together now rather than fighting.

Everyone has witnessed or heard a story just like this one, about a time when God answered a desperate call. The point is simple: God doesn't have to prove His love for us, but that doesn't stop Him from blessing us. Our faith in Him, our investment in His kingdom, is always justified.

This doesn't mean that God always gives us what we want, or that if we tithe, we will receive every single thing we pray for. Tithing is not like buying a pair of pants on Amazon.com; we don't offer money to God and receive what we order in just the right size and color. In some ways, our relationship with money can confuse our expectations. After all, money is of this world—it's tangible, measurable. A dollar will get you a hamburger at McDonald's; three dollars buys a gallon of milk. God, however, works in mysterious ways, and we don't get to see His menu. He probably doesn't even *have* a menu to begin with—but He does have a perfect plan.

As such, we often aren't ready to, as the saying goes, "put our money where our mouth is." The real truth is that a lot of us—maybe even most of us—simply have a lack of faith. We don't believe God is who He says is and that He will take care of us, despite what we say out loud and how often we come to church. We believe in God, of course, that He's up there and cares about us.

In our deepest hearts, however, we wonder if He cares enough to impact our daily lives and create the change we're praying for. But what is it that leads us to think this? Pastors? Misunderstood teachings or passages? Our own expectations of what God should do?

We have all been guilty of hearing a sermon or reading a Scripture passage and only focusing on the part that sounds good. We then expect God to respond in a certain way, and when He doesn't, we doubt His love for us. Maybe, because God answered a prayer the way we expected in the past, we anticipate He will do that again, not realizing He has answered according to His will. We are not recognizing the big picture or God's answer when it comes, because we don't always see His perfect plan.

God executes His plan, not ours. And frankly, sometimes what we want is not good for us. Parents with children know this all too well (and we are all, in a sense, God's children). Kids love to negotiate and promise us things, thinking they can manipulate us to give them whatever they want. They don't understand that parents often see the world in a different way and can see dangers their kids aren't aware of.

Our relationship with God is the same way. We pray, asking for certain things, and try to negotiate with God. We tell God we will stop doing this behavior or that behavior if only He will grant us our wish. Sometimes we might even give more in the offering with an impure, greedy motive that God will then automatically give us more. However, God is not a God of negotiation. He truly knows what is best for us, and He will not give us anything out of His will for us.

We should not tithe in the hopes of earning God's goodwill, but as a statement of our commitment, an investment in His promise and plan for the future.

So, What Does God Promise?

We need look no further than the book of Psalms to understand what God has in store for us. Here we will find many of God's promises to us:

> Trust in the LORD, and do good; so shalt thou dwell in the land, and verily thou shalt be fed.
> —*Psalm 37:3 (KJV)*

God offers us abundance, though not the kind we may be expecting. God's abundance is not the reality-TV kind, where young, rich men and women receive fancy cars, designer clothes, and other extravagant gifts from their parents. His plan is not to spoil us with all sorts of material things. God doesn't promise us five houses and multimillion-dollar sports contracts or record deals. He doesn't promise us material wealth, but He has given us a beautiful world in which to live.

Too often, we think of "God's abundance" as having riches or worldly possessions, and we don't appreciate the things He has already blessed us with. But God's abundance is so much more than material things, and it is visible all around us if we just look around.

Before God even created man, He prepared an incredible world for us (Genesis 1:1–27). He made the wondrous earth and then gave it all to us.

> God blessed them and said to them, "Be fruitful and increase in number; fill the earth and subdue it. Rule over the fish in the sea and the birds in the sky and over every living creature that moves on the ground."
>
> Then God said, "I give you every seed-bearing plant on the face of the whole earth and every tree that has fruit with seed in it. They will be yours for food. And to all the beasts of the earth and all the birds in the sky and all the creatures that move along the ground—everything that has the breath of life in it—I give every green plant for food." And it was so.
>
> **—Genesis 1:28–30**

From the trees in our neighborhood, to the highest mountains, the fish that live in the sea, and every sunset—we can enjoy God's abundance in every moment of our lives.

God didn't stop at giving us the beautiful world He created or supplying our food and other basic needs. Abundance is not only about where we live, what we do for work, the food we eat, our bank account, or a vehicle that runs. God wants so much more for us. He also blesses us with wisdom, peace, understanding, and yes, the provision we need to execute what He's called us to do.

God desires us to seek Him so that He can bless us with these things. When we commit ourselves to being in His presence, studying His Word, and praying, God gives us abundance. You can't put a price on wisdom, peace, and the understanding we can only receive from Him.

The Bible says, "Delight yourself in the LORD, and he will give you the desires of your heart" (Psalm 37:4 ESV). When we spend time trying to be more like Him and doing His things His way, then our desires will mesh with His and this psalm becomes real in our lives.

God enjoys giving us prosperity—whether that be material, emotional, or spiritual blessing—but He doesn't automatically do it. When we are following the Lord and living according to His ways, He blesses us with this prosperity. Many Christians assume that the prosperity is automatic, but God's Word says otherwise.

> Blessed is the one who does not walk in step with the wicked or stand in the way that sinners take or sit in the company of mockers, but whose delight is in the law of the LORD, and who meditates on his law day and night. That person is like a tree planted by streams of water, which yields its fruit in season and whose leaf does not wither—

whatever they do prospers.
                                    —Psalm 1:1–3

He also promises us favor, as Psalm 5:11 tell us: "But let all who take refuge in you be glad; let them ever sing for joy. Spread your protection over them, that those who love your name may rejoice in you."

Favor, in this case, means that God raises His followers up through their own abilities. He shows us how to use our gifts and talents, our resources and influence, to find our way out of difficulties. More importantly, He shows us how to use these gifts and talents for His kingdom.

Choosing to Believe in Him

Now that we understand what God has promised, we are faced with a very simple decision: Will we trust Him?

To answer that question, we need to understand the nature of trust, which can be a funny thing. Those whom we choose to trust can be even funnier. The late Maya Angelou once said, "When someone shows you who they are, believe them."[2] In other words, the best way to determine whether someone is trustworthy or not is through their actions. Whether we realize it or not, this is already the way we pick our friends. People come into our lives and earn our trust over time by fulfilling their promises, by doing what they say they will. We develop a kind of faith in their integrity, strength, and abilities that draws us closer to them.

In other cases, trust is implicit. We are born trusting our parents, grandparents, and other close family members. From a young age, we are also taught to trust teachers, coaches, and other authority figures. Strangely, we sometimes choose to put our faith in people we've never even met before—athletes, singers, or movie stars. There's something powerful about seeing these people on TV or on magazine covers. It gives them a strange "glow" that we may interpret as wisdom. We're always hungry for wisdom, and, as such, we can easily be fooled.

Most worrisome of all, we tend to trust institutions. We put our money into banks and 401Ks and expect our savings to grow. We trust the companies we work for to keep our jobs secure, and we trust our government to rule fairly, despite evidence that oftentimes these systems betray us.

In all these cases, from our parents right on down the line, our trust continues to grow and develop—unless it is broken by betrayal. We've all dealt with the pain of that feeling and the way it lingers for a very long time. Maybe it was a close friend who spilled a secret, a boyfriend or girlfriend who cheated on us, or a relative who stabbed us in the back. Maybe it was an unhealthy relationship to begin with and we should not have trusted the person. All relationships—both good and bad—can affect how we respond to trusting God. We can't base our trust on man's good deeds or their failings.

There are less personal but equally traumatic examples as well: people who have lost their retirement accounts when the stock market crashed or their pensions when their company folded. In every case, we must decide to work and repair that trust, or if the pain is too great, we allow it to remain broken forever.

Where does God come into play in all of this? He is responsible for all the blessings in our lives. He never betrays us, not even when we turn our back on Him. Yet we often fail to show Him that we recognize and appreciate His many blessings. Often, we may forget Him entirely when things are going well, only to drop back onto our knees and beg for help the next time we find ourselves in trouble.

But when I am afraid, I will put my trust in you. I praise God for what he has promised. I trust in God, so why should I be afraid? What can mere mortals do to me?
—Psalm 56: 3–4 *(NLT)*

We don't tithe to earn God's favor, to bribe Him for better fortune or more wealth. Nor are we paying a "tax" on the blessings He has already bestowed. We do this to show God that we are grateful for His generosity and mercy. We do it to show that we trust in Him and His promises.

By trusting in God, we know He has our best interest at heart when He responds to our prayers. We can be confident that He will grow our seeds of faith and show us why He is worthy to be praised.

WORKBOOK

Chapter Two Questions

Question: Describe a time in your life when, like Elijah and the widow of Zarephath, you experienced God's miraculous or unexpected provision. How did this experience build your faith?

_____

_____

_____

_____

_____

_____

_____

_____

_____

_____

Question: What are some of the non-material things that make up God's abundance toward you? How do you (or how could you) express appreciation for these expressions of His abundance?

_____

_____

_____

_____

_____

_____

_____

_____

_____

_____

Question: How would you encourage a friend who is trying their best to follow biblical commands and principles, yet is experiencing financial hardship? What verses might apply to this person's situation?

_____

_____

_____

_____

_____

_____

_____

_____

_____

_____

_____

_____

Action: What does it mean to you, personally, that God can be trusted? Write out several examples of times in your life when you saw God come through for you and provide what you needed at just the right time (include the example you gave in response to the first question). Review these special stories of God's faithfulness when you are tempted to doubt. Share at least one of these stories with at least one other person this week. If you have a child (or children), remember to share these stories with them, in particular, so that they will learn to see God's faithfulness.

Chapter Two Notes

_____

_____

_____

_____

_____

_____

_____

_____

_____

_____

_____

_____

_____

_____

_____

_____

_____

_____

_____

_____

_____

CHAPTER THREE

To Sow *and* To Reap

In the Sermon on the Mount, Jesus drew a line between serving God and serving greed, between choosing His kingdom and choosing the world of man. But because we live every day of our lives in the world of man, it can be hard to break free enough to consistently choose God's kingdom. Building our faith and serving God is a continual, intentional process, one that takes much time and work. The first step is learning to sow.

Back in biblical times, much more so than today, men were farmers. Their lives were a constant cycle of seasons, harvest and planting and harvest again. Farmers know better than anyone that you don't keep everything from the harvest. You have to set some seed aside to sow in the next planting season.

Tithing is a form of sowing. The only difference is, we don't plant the seeds in our gardens, but in God's through our churches and other ministries. "Honor the LORD with your wealth, with the firstfruits of all your crops; then your barns will be filled to overflowing, and your vats will brim over with new wine" (Proverbs 3:9–10).

For those who want to begin giving, the easiest place to start is by asking God for help, the same way we seek His guidance in other matters in our lives. God knows your heart and your circumstances. If He is asking you to give, then listen to Him and do it. Our perception of our ability to faithfully give should not be a factor. Ignore the voice in your head trying to persuade you to keep everything for yourself. It may be the devil's voice or your own.

Though we are made in God's image and likeness, we remain imperfect since being cast out of the Garden of Eden (Genesis 1:27). Our imperfections lead us to fill our lives with the things of this world, diversions and distractions that we hope will satisfy us.

This is a real problem today. In this country, we have more "stuff" than ever before, even the poorest among us. It's not only rich people walking around with fancy cell phones. The technology just keeps getting better; every week new products come out—better TVs, smaller tablets, new channels and movies and shows. We devote so much time to this entertainment, but it doesn't make us feel any happier. If anything, we feel even more lonely; the holes within us seem to get deeper the more we fill them with material things.

The Lord knows what really matters, and He's trying to tell us what that is. Trust in Him—He will not lead you astray (Provers 3:5–6). Sometimes we forget how much He cares about us. We think our connection to Him comes only later, when we're safely tucked away in heaven. We create an equation just as we do with money: Following God means getting into heaven. But He is not a genie that we ignore until we die and then are granted the wish of eternal life. He cares about our lives, about us, *now*. God wants us to be obedient to Him at any cost, so that we may enjoy His many blessings.

To tithe is to put God first—it is a reflection of the posture of our hearts. There's a difference between not tithing finances because of whittling away money and struggling to survive and merely holding back because you don't trust God or His command to give.

The reality is that sometimes uncontrollable circumstances may put you in a position where your budget is tight. And sometimes you may have to step out in faith to tithe. This could be due to death, joblessness, illness, or many other factors.

Our goal is simply to avoid the path of our friend Lucy, whom we met earlier in the book. The woman who came into some money and then instantly wiled most of it away before she even considered God or His kingdom. We need to give to Him our "firstfruits" (Deuteronomy 26:2), rather than offer Him our last few scraps—especially when God blesses us with extra money.

This means making a commitment to put aside your tithe right away and trusting Him to provide the rest of what you need. Perhaps you have enough for the rest of your needs and then some after a tithe, or maybe you have to rework your entire budget with your tithe in mind. The point is, you are committing to give to God *first*.

There will always be temptations: the latest, coolest gadget, a trip to Vegas with friends, or an expensive dinner at a steakhouse with your spouse. It's perfectly fine to enjoy yourself—God wants you to celebrate your harvest—but don't forget about Him in the process.

Finally, remember to take care of His house as well as your own. We all want a nice living space, however big or small. But while you are furnishing your home with nice carpets, curtains, and appliances, be sure not to neglect God's house. Think of it in the same way you think of your own. God desires the best from us, and that includes how we care for His house. We should treat God's house with reverence and respect.

Giving Is a Privilege

Commitment to tithing means choosing God's system over that of the world. We're used to the way things work in the world; we understand the power of money and credit cards and interest rates. But God's system has an entirely different focus. He wants us to give without thinking of the payback.

He understands, however, that *we* care about money. Luke 12:34 says: "For where your treasure is, there your heart will be also." In other words, the best way to tell what people value is to observe how they spend their money. The truth of this is obvious when we consider our own patterns of behavior. Some people prefer an expensive car, that BMW or Lexus, while others are content to get around town in the same beat-up Honda they've had since college. Some people spring for a fancy hotel on vacation and others stay in hostels because they only need a clean bed and a place to shower. The list could go on forever, but the point is clear: Money reveals our priorities in the same way that voting reveals our politics.

Choosing to tithe sends a powerful message that God matters to us, that our churches matter to us, and, most important of all, that other people matter to us. By offering a sacrifice after our harvest, we declare that we are givers. It's our way of acknowledging the blessings God has bestowed on us and expressing our willingness to use those blessings to help others. Through tithing, we demonstrate to God that we earnestly desire to invest capital in His kingdom. This is

how we become what Paul calls "cheerful givers." And as he reminds us in 2 Corinthians 9:7,
"God loves a cheerful giver."

We are meant to share what we have so that
God can use us to bless others and point them to
Jesus. One of the first things we teach our children is how to share, whether it be with an older
or younger sibling or another child at the park.
Kids aren't born wanting to share. As much as we
like to think of our babies as precious little angels,
we spend enough time with them to know better.
They aren't perfect, which is why good role mod-
els are so important. A parent's job is to educate
their child—in many ways, to civilize their child.
We tell them, "You have these toys over here.
Why don't you let your little brother or sister play
with this one?"

Every parent in the world has said those words
at one time or another, but somehow, we fail to
apply the message to ourselves. Giving is a privilege afforded to us because we have bounty to
offer. It's also a spiritual test, one of those defin-
ing moments that reveals our convictions. Saying
what we believe is easy; it's through our actions
that we truly show ourselves. More than this, actions are the way in which we shape our character.

And what is character? By the simplest defini-
tion, *character* is following through on
commitments, proving that we are men and
women of our word. It's one of our greatest ide-
als, what we look for in our very best leaders and

politicians. Dr. Martin Luther King Jr. said it best when he wished for a world in which people are judged "by the content of their character."[3] There can be no higher standard.

We say we believe in God, that we trust His plan for us and commit to His system rather than our own. Giving affords us a way to prove this. And by doing so, we also show who we are and that we value God's kingdom and the things He values.

Preparing for New Challenges

Once we understand what giving really means, we may feel uncomfortable with what we have to offer. Some people may wonder if the little they have to give serves any purpose at all: How much could five or ten dollars possibly matter? But the Bible is full of countless stories of small things having a huge impact.

In John 6:1–14, Jesus and His apostles were once again standing on top of a mountain looking down on a multitude of people who came to hear Him preach. As the day wore on, the apostles became concerned because they had no money or food enough for a crowd of thousands. Andrew told Jesus that a small boy had five loaves of bread and two small fish—certainly not enough to feed so many people.

Jesus, of course, was not worried. He offered a prayer for the food before the apostles began to distribute it to the crowd. They were amazed to find that not only was everyone fed, but twelve baskets of leftovers remained afterward. It's worth keeping this story in mind when we worry that what we have to offer won't do any good. God has done more with less before.

Other challenges also await us once we commit to giving. Sometimes the devil may challenge us, to try to knock us from this new path we've chosen. Imagine a young couple that becomes inspired by the Holy Spirit and decides to buy groceries for a poor family in their parish. They drop the food off and feel very good about themselves because they're doing God's work. Then, out of nowhere, on the drive home, their car breaks down. Now this couple faces unexpected (and expensive) repairs! They could really use some of that money they have just spent on someone else's groceries.

The devil likes to pull these kinds of tricks. He doesn't want us looking out for our neighbors or demonstrating a commitment to God's system over that of man's, which he has helped pervert. The devil wants us wasting our money. He wants us to spend $500 on useless stuff because he knows what we'll get: $500 worth of nothing that matters.

It might also be that God Himself tests us when we start to give. Maybe God wants us to show Him what we do and don't value. Do we trust Him to keep His promises and provide for us when we step out in faith? God often challenges His people because He understands, even if we don't, that this is how we grow our faith.

Everyone knows the story of Abraham and Isaac (Genesis 22:1–18). God commanded Abraham to sacrifice his own son as an offering to Him. Not a weekly donation in the collection basket, not ten percent of his salary, but his *only* child.

Abraham didn't even hesitate. He took his son into the desert and started building an altar. When God sent an angel down to stop him, Abraham had already pulled out his knife to do the deed!

"'Do not lay a hand on the boy,' he said. 'Do not do anything to him. Now I know that you fear God, because you have not withheld from me your son, your only son'" (Genesis 22:12). In other words, God said through His angel, "Okay, okay, you've proven your faith. Now put down the knife—let's not get crazy."

God put Abraham through what's called a "sovereign test," which can be about money, our attitude, or our obedience. He drops these tests on us from time to time, and we respond in different ways—not always the right way, either. When God told Jonah to journey to Nineveh, Jonah flat-out refused (Jonah 3–4). "They're sinners," he said. "They don't need to be saved. They don't deserve this mercy. Sorry, God, I'm not going." Jonah abandoned his responsibilities and ended up in the belly of a huge fish for his troubles.

These examples of Abraham's and Jonah's tests remind me of a personal story from several years ago. I was at a prayer conference when the Lord told me to give what was a sacrificial amount at the time. I had $700 in my bank account, and He told me to give $500. I had doubts creep in—that was almost everything I had! *"Where would my food come from? How would I pay my bills?"* I was nervous, but I listened to Him. That day I set a precedence—I would be obedient to Him no matter what He asked of me because I trusted His faithfulness.

Whether God tests us through asking us to give money we don't think we have, doing something radical that makes no sense, or following Him when we don't know the outcome, He will bless us when we obey. God does not need our money; He needs our hearts.

God's sovereign tests for us don't end when we choose to tithe. In every trial, we can choose to respond like Abraham or like Jonah did, with obedience and faith or with flight. But by choosing to give, we reveal in the clearest possible terms where—and to whom—our allegiance lies. We also serve as an example to our families, friends, and even complete strangers that it's possible to live in the world of man while staying focused on the Kingdom of God.

WORKBOOK

Chapter Three Questions

Question: In what ways is giving like sowing seed? How is faith required for both giving and sowing? Describe the harvest that comes from faithful giving.

_____

_____

_____

_____

_____

_____

_____

_____

_____

_____

_____

Question: What does your giving say about your priorities? How does learning to give shape your character?

_____

_____

_____

_____

_____

_____

_____

_____

_____

_____

Question: What are some of the challenges and hindrances you may face regarding giving? How can you stay faithful in the face of these obstacles?

_____

_____

_____

_____

_____

_____

_____

_____

_____

_____

_____

Action: *Giving is a privilege.* Have you ever faced a time when you could not give a gift to your spouse, children, or someone else you love? List some of the thoughts and emotions associated with the inability to give. Then write out *"Giving is a privilege because…"* and list several reasons why this is true. Remind yourself of the privileges of giving next time you are struggling to share your blessings with others.

Chapter Three Notes

CHAPTER FOUR

Investing in God's Plan

Tithing expresses our intention to prioritize God's plan over our worldly goals and ambitions. But the truth is, we have more than money to give, and the Lord wants it all. There's an expression that started in the game of poker, but people use it all the time nowadays: *all-in.* In the game, players go "all-in" when they decide to bet all their chips on one particular hand.

God wants us to go all-in with our faith, too. He wants us to invest, not just a portion of our income through tithing, but everything we have— all of our gifts and talents. He asks us to be contributors to His kingdom, not just consumers, and creators, not just caretakers. God wants real voices, not echoes.

Sometimes people only think of giving as a monetary issue. However, we often overlook how giving our time is an investment in God's kingdom as well. God's plan is that people come to

Him. We can further His kingdom when we serve at church, show love to those who don't think they need it, encourage one another, pray for one another, and do things to bless others.

> *For we are God's handiwork, created in Christ Jesus to do good works, which God prepared in advance for us to do.*
> **—Ephesians 2:10**

God created each of us uniquely and has a plan for us (Ephesians 2:10). The way God wishes to use me will be different from how He plans to use you. God has equipped us perfectly to do the things He has for each of us. This includes any talents and gifts He has given us.

We have unique talents that can transform our faith communities if we have the courage to unlock them. Oftentimes, however, we don't. We have faith in God but little in ourselves—in the gifts and talents He has placed within us.

> *God's various gifts are handed out everywhere; but they all originate in God's Spirit. God's various ministries are carried out everywhere; but they all originate in God's Spirit. God's various expressions of power are in action everywhere; but God himself is behind it all. Each person is given something to do that shows who God is: Everyone gets in on it, everyone benefits.*

*All kinds of things are handed out by the Spirit,
and to all kinds of people!*
—1 Corinthians 12:4–10 (MSG)

In other words, all our different talents come from God, not chance. Too many of us fail to grasp what this means. We make weak, nervous attempts to use our talents and then we quit at the first taste of failure. We don't realize that success is almost always borne of failure. Very few people in the history of the world succeed on their first attempt.

Imagine what we can achieve if we trust in our abilities and the talents that we have kept hidden from our neighbors, even from our closest friends and family. The truth is, we want blessings, but we fail to understand they are often the fruit of labor and faith. God doesn't always give us blessings in their final form; sometimes He offers us the seeds that will become blessings once we have put in the necessary effort. That is, God didn't offer today's top song artists multimillion-dollar record deals. Rather, He gave them a beautiful voice and talent they developed to *earn* those record deals.

The Lord expects from us a return on His investment of talents and abilities. Most people will never be music stars—we aren't all meant for fame and fortune. But we do all have gifts, and we will find fulfillment in using those gifts for His kingdom. Some people are wonderful painters or builders; others are great with numbers, and a lucky few are born leaders. Every one of those abilities has a place in God's plan.

Our commitment to Him doesn't end with a tithe dropped into the collection basket. We need to invest everything we have, to go "all-in" with the talents, hard work, and dedication He has given us, and allow His blessings to bear fruit. Going all-in isn't just about using those talents in the church. When others see us working as unto the Lord in our jobs or using our talents to bless other people, then they can see how God has blessed us and how we are giving back.

Taking the First Step Out of the Boat

When we use our talents, we don't always know how God will use them to increase our faith or the faith of others. When Moses stood before the Lord saying, "I am slow of speech and tongue" (Exodus 4:10), he had no idea how God would use him to be a great leader. Moses stepped out and obeyed, and God used him to change history.

People have done things nearly as impossible throughout our history. Harriet Tubman was a slave before she saved hundreds of people just like herself using the Underground Railroad. Mary McLeod Bethune's parents were slaves. She went on to start a private school for black students, and President Roosevelt made her one of his national advisors. People called her "the First Lady of the Struggle."[4]

We can use the talents and abilities God has given us to walk on water. In Matthew 14:22–31, the apostles were waiting for Jesus on a boat as He prayed alone following a long day of preaching. The sun went down and the sea started to grow rough. Finally, the apostles spotted Jesus— He was walking toward them *on the water.* It was so spooky that they convinced themselves it must have been a ghost.

When Jesus told them it was Him, Peter said, "Lord, if it's you … tell me to come to you on the water" (Matthew 14:28). And that's just what Jesus did. The other apostles watched in shock as Peter started walking on the water, too—until he lost faith. The wind picked up, and Peter got nervous; he looked down at the water and immediately started to sink. Jesus, of course, was right there to save him. He reached out a hand and saved Peter before asking him, "You of little faith…. Why did you doubt?" (Matthew 14:31).

It's a question that applies to many of us today as we continue to squander the talents we could be using to serve God better. We, too, need to be willing to leave the safety and comfort of our boats and join the Lord. The good news is, our first step is a lot easier than Peter's. Instead of trying to walk on water, all we need to do is commit to working harder at pursuing God's plans.

Talents take training. We need look no further than the military for proof of this fact. The military has prestigious academies like West Point to school their officers. West Point takes the very best recruits, identifies their talents, and then hones them. It's an intense process, and there are no shortcuts.

A lot of people don't like to hear this—they prefer shortcuts and easy outs. Processes take time and effort, trial and error, and most of all, doubt. Peter experienced this when he stepped out of the boat and onto the water. His first few steps were no problem. Then the wind started howling and he thought, *"This is impossible—I'm not supposed to walk on water. I'm about to drown out here."*

It was only when he doubted that Peter began to sink. We can learn from Peter's mistake. Instead of doubting—and sinking—we can choose to trust God in these moments when the devil is whispering like the wind in our ear that we can't do this, that we're kidding ourselves. By turning to Him in prayer, we can tune the devil out. God is always right beside us, just as Jesus was right beside Peter on the water that night. And He has given us what we need to succeed in life.

Keep Going

Once there was a man named Larry who worked for a bishop, but Larry had a very serious drug addiction. The bishop put Larry in a program, and it helped him get clean. Of course, the addiction had left Larry's life in shambles, with few places to turn. But this man never gave up, and because of that, he just kept moving up. He became a deacon and eventually earned an architect's degree; now he designs buildings and makes a very good living on the strength of his own talents and abilities.

God didn't gift Larry with wealth or riches, but He showed the man the way out of his darkness by using what was already inside him.

Not all of us are meant to change history, but we all have a role to play in God's plan. Our talents can be just as great an investment as our tithes if they are used to their full potential. We must keep working, keep honing our special gifts. To quit, to wave the white flag of surrender, is to turn our back on God, the One who gave them to us in the first place. Keep moving forward and using the gifts God has given you, and watch Him use your life for His glory.

WORKBOOK

Chapter Four Questions

Question: What does it mean to be "all in" for God? What gifts, talents, and abilities has God given you, and how can you use them for Him?

_____

_____

_____

_____

_____

_____

_____

_____

_____

_____

_____

Question: Why do people sometimes hide their talent or give up on serving God? What raw abilities do you have that could be developed through time and perseverance? What steps do you need to take?

_____

_____

_____

_____

_____

_____

_____

_____

_____

_____

_____

Question: What should a Christian's attitude be toward fame and fortune? Give examples of Christian people who have used their fame and/or fortune well, as well as some who (apparently) have not.

_____

_____

_____

_____

_____

_____

_____

_____

_____

_____

_____

_____

Action #1: Talk to a trusted friend or a career counselor about how you can best utilize the inherent abilities and aptitude God has given you. Do you have a clear career path? If not, start to develop one. How can you maximize your current opportunities?

Action #2: Read a biography of one of the people mentioned in this chapter or of another well-known Christian who impacted the church and culture. How did this person overcome obstacles and keep persevering when the task seemed impossible? How did they develop their natural, God-given talents and abilities to be of maximum usefulness?

Chapter Four Notes

_____

_____

_____

_____

_____

_____

_____

_____

_____

_____

_____

_____

_____

_____

_____

_____

_____

_____

_____

_____

_____

_____

CONCLUSION

Choose to Trust

But blessed is the one who trusts in the LORD, *whose confidence is in him. They will be like a tree planted by the water that sends out its roots by the stream. It does not fear when heat comes; its leaves are always green. It has no worries in a year of drought and never fails to bear fruit.*
—Jeremiah 17:7–8

As Christians, we have a choice to trust in God's plan, to commit to His kingdom even as we make our way through this world of material things. A tithe is a symbol of this choice. We often "vote with our wallets" to show what really matters to us; by tithing, we are prioritizing God and the well-being of our neighbors over ourselves.

Giving is also a privilege, a joyful acknowledgment of the harvest the Lord has bestowed upon us. Just as we teach our children to share, so we must learn the same lesson, often in the face of significant temptations. God's system is far different from that of the world; we face pressures at every turn to indulge our own greed rather than give back.

A tithe sends the message that God is worthy of our trust. Unlike many of the people and institutions with which we surround ourselves, He never abandons or betrays us.

But having faith in God and His plan is not without its challenges. He asks much of us, not simply a share of the blessings He's bestowed, but the fruits of our talents and abilities, as well. The Lord challenges us to invest wholly of ourselves because ultimately, we are His seeds, put here to grow and multiply and then be harvested as He sees fit.

With this encouraging truth in mind, choose today to commit every aspect of your life to God. Learn to trust Him completely—and choose to love generously!

Conclusion Action Step

Action: Talk to your pastor about a financial management course that he would recommend. There are many excellent resources from a Christian perspective. Learn wise principles of money management and begin to put them into practice so that you will be able to give intentionally and specifically while still providing for the needs of your own family and saving for the future.

REFERENCES

Notes

1. Dayton, Howard L. Jr. *Leadership* (Spring 1981), p. 62.

2. Angelou, Maya. In "One of the Most Important Lessons Dr. Maya Angelou Ever Taught Oprah: The Oprah Winfrey Show," YouTube video, posted by OWN, May 19, 2014. https://www.youtube.com/watch?v=nJgmaHkcFP8.

3. King, Martin Luther Jr. "I Have a Dream." Speech. Lincoln Memorial, Washington, D.C. August 28, 1963.

4. "Mary McLeod Bethune Biography" *Biography*.com. April 2, 2014. https://www.biography.com/people/mary-mcleod-bethune-9211266.

Acknowledgments

I give honor and thanks to God for His saving power and for His Holy Spirit, who is within me—teaching me and guiding me through everyday life and leading me to start and finish projects like *Live Generously.*

Thanks to my beautiful wife, Lady Glynis, for your steadfastness and continued support and dedication throughout the years. My life would not be what it is without you. Thank you for your prayers, support, and assistance on this project.

Thanks to my children—Anthony Jr., Kendra, and Ba'lint Shannon. I am so proud of you. Each one of you is following the course that God, your mother, and I have developed for you. I am excited about what God is doing in your life, and I am in continual expectation of what God is doing to you, for you, and in you. I know and believe the best is yet to come in your lives. Remember the Shannon Creed: *"Represent the Shannons Well and Bring Glory to God!"*

Thanks to Dr. R.A. Vernon and Lady Vernon, who poured into Lady Shannon and me, for teaching me how to love (and hug) on every member and visitor who attends our services and for encouraging us in writing and doing Matthew 25 Alive.

Thanks to Bishop I.V. and Lady Bridget Hilliard, who introduced me to systematic faith and taught me that I could have God's best, both spiritually and materially. You helped me understand that whatever is possible for me is according to my faith. And thank you for creating the AIM organization, where I have met some incredible men and women of God.

Thanks to my mother, Sharon Shannon, who has prayed for me, laid hands on me, and encouraged me so that I would follow the will of God and fulfill my purpose in life. Thanks also to my late Aunt Patricia and Uncle William Gibson for their many years of encouragement and for allowing me to teach them the gospel and practice my preaching on them.

I owe special thanks to the wonderful congregation of The Victory Church International in Westland, Michigan. A church is only as great as the members who are a part of it, which is why I am proud to say: *you are a great church!* You are truly living the Jesus leadership style—*love.* Thank you for being committed to the vision. I've told you before, but let me say it again, that I deeply appreciate you allowing me to be your pastor. Always know that your pastor prophet loves you!

Finally, thanks to Marcus and Beth Jenkins and Morgan Phillips for being partners with my ministry and for their encouragement. You have been catalysts to push me forward—planting the many seeds, seeing this revelation of seedtime and harvest come to pass, and manifesting this project: ***Live Generously!***

About the Author

Anthony D. Shannon is the founder and senior pastor of The Victory Church International, in Westland, Michigan. He is a licensed and ordained pastor of the gospel of our Lord Jesus Christ. As a servant leader teaching the Jesus leadership style, he loves to say, "I *get* to serve, I don't *have* to serve."

His ministry began on October 1, 1989, when he had a life-changing experience with God Almighty. God called him into the ministry and said, "Anthony, I am calling you to be a preacher, teacher, and a prophet to the nation, and you will be known for your accuracy in the prophetic. I will make your name great, and you will handle millions of dollars." Since this conversation, Anthony Shannon has labored in the gospel wholeheartedly to eat, sleep, and drink the Word of God and to become one with it.

Prophet Shannon is a native to Detroit, Michigan. He is deeply committed to sharing the Word of God with revelation and passion. His desire to preach and teach the Word with accuracy had led him to study biblical scholars, Jewish rabbis, and some top minds who proclaim Jesus Christ as Lord and savior.

He holds a bachelor's degree in business administration as well as a Master of Divinity degree. He is president and founder of God's Gear Gospel Wear (Christian clothing line) and MGM-P (community development corporation), and he is the founder of The Giver's Club, a non-profit that gives away free gifts to bless others.

In addition, Prophet Shannon can be seen hosting television shows on TCT Network, Detroit: *TCT Alive*, *Michigan Alive*, and *Ask the Pastor*. He also has his own show, called *Managing God's Money Properly*, and hosts a radio show, *The Prophetic Knights*, on 1340AM. By email, he sends *The Dose of Encouragement Weekly* to hundreds of leaders, pastors, bishops, and apostles.

Prophet Shannon is well known and recognized for his accuracy in the prophetic gift. The top prophets of our day have certified Anthony

Shannon as a true authenticated prophet of our day: Bill Harmon, John Paul Jackson, Francina Norman, E. Bernard Jordon, Robert Rejoice, Michael Jones, and of course, Jesus Christ. He has spoken prophetically into the lives of many men and women of God, who have confirmed the accuracy and the authenticity of his prophecies. He has over 10,000 hours of training in the prophetic and is a certified master/senior prophet.

He is the founder of Prophetic Knights—a monthly gathering that focuses on teaching people from the prophetic and prophesying as the Spirit leads. He has been recognized for his accomplishments in the *Who's Who in Black Detroit*, *Detroit Free Press*, *Michigan Chronicle*, *Black Detroit Magazine*, *Connection Magazine*, *Detroit News*, *Retail Magazine*, and *Insights Magazine*.

Prophet Shannon was installed as Pastor of Beyond the Veil International Christian Center by Bishop William Murphy Jr. of New Mount Mariah Baptist Church in Pontiac, Michigan. He has faithfully served with the Full Gospel Baptist Church Fellowship as armor bearer to Bishop Murphy, and as an elder and servant leader under Bishop Murphy, since 1991. In 1997, he was selected to be the first assistant to Bishop Michael Jones for the FGBCF Ministerial Alliance. Prophet Shannon now serves as the director of education for the FGBCF at the state level (with Bishop Devay Myatt) and at the international level (with Bishop Cheryl Brown).

He also serves the community in several capacities. He is a commander chaplain for the Detroit Police Chaplain Corps, a chaplain for the Wayne County Sheriff's Department, and a member of the International Fellowship of Chaplains.

Prophet Shannon is a member of the Association of Independent Ministries. In 2005, he was ordained as a pastor by the New Light Church and the Association of Independent Ministries, under the direction of Bishop I.V. and Dr. Bridget Hilliard of New Light Christian Center Church in Houston, Texas. Prophet Shannon is also associated with the Destiny Outreach Ministry Association, the Shepherds Connection, and the Champions Network.

In 2015, he became a certified international trainer, coach, and speaker to business leaders and others through the John Maxwell International Training Program, where is he called to raise up future leaders.

Prophet Shannon has become a sought-after speaker to the body of Christ and to the business world as a pastor, apostolic teacher, and senior prophet of the Lord Jesus Christ. He is an author who proclaims the gospel of Jesus Christ and the Kingdom of God. He shares a blessed life with his lovely wife, Glynis, and three children: Anthony Jr., Kendra Diana, and Ba'lint, all of whom he loves very much.

www.ingramcontent.com/pod-product-compliance
Lightning Source LLC
LaVergne TN
LVHW051426080426
835508LV00022B/3264